CONTENTS

Get in the race!

Imagine your feet on the pedals. You zip around corners. You land jumps like Olympic gold medalists Connor Fields and Mariana Pajón. Bicycle Motocross, or BMX, racing is popular all over the world. It's full of action, sharp turns and lots of jumps. Grab your helmet and get ready to ride!

FROM PRETEND TO PRO RACER

Scot Breithaupt is the founder of BMX. At the age of 13, he and his friends rode their bikes on an empty patch of wasteland. They pretended to race. The game caught on and grew into BMX racing.

FACT

BMX racing officially became an Olympic sport in 2008. There are men's and women's competitions.

CONNOR FIELDS

"I know I might be biased, but I think BMX is so cool and one of the best sports in the world!"

– *BMX gold medalist Connor Fields*

CHAPTER 1
Get ready to ride!

Equipment

BMX bikes are like ordinary bikes with a few changes. They have small **frames**. BMX bikes usually have 51-centimetre (20-inch) wheels. Most have only one **gear** and one brake. Because BMX bikes are used for racing, they are made of light metals, such as aluminium. A lighter bike can go faster.

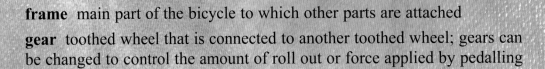

FACT
Most professional or Olympic BMX races last less than 1 minute. Races for beginners may take longer.

frame main part of the bicycle to which other parts are attached

gear toothed wheel that is connected to another toothed wheel; gears can be changed to control the amount of roll out or force applied by pedalling

Safety equipment

BMX racing involves high speeds and jumps. It is important to have the right safety equipment. An ordinary cycling helmet isn't enough. For BMX racing you need a full helmet that protects your head and face. Safety goggles protect your eyes from flying rocks and dirt. Gloves, kneepads and elbow pads can protect you during **wipeouts**.

FACT

BMX riders must have at least an approved helmet, long-sleeved top and trousers. Elbow pads and body armour give added protection, but they are not required.

wipeout fall or crash

The track

BMX racing tracks are usually made of dirt. They have many jumps and turns. The **starting gate** is at the top of a large ramp or hill. Riders use this to build up speed for the race. Many tracks have three sharp turns. They look like a giant "M" or "W" from above.

starting gate place where a race starts; the gate has room for eight riders and ensures that all riders get a fair start

CHAPTER 2

How the race works

Competitors

A BMX race has three separate parts called motos. The best riders in each moto advance to the next one.

Each rider sits at his or her own starting gate to begin. Riders compete in two or three **qualification heats**. The top eight racers compete for first place.

FACT
There may be more or fewer qualification heats depending on how many riders are competing.

qualification heat one of several early races that determine which riders advance to future qualifying rounds or the main event

Obstacles

A BMX track is full of **obstacles**. Rollers are small bumps in the track. They may be grouped together to form a bumpy "rhythm" section that slows down riders. A step-up is a small hill followed by a larger hill. A step-down is a large hill followed by a smaller hill.

obstacle something a BMX rider jumps or rides over

Riders try to get through obstacles quickly. The track is set up to help them. A tabletop jump has a flat top. Riders can land on top if they can't jump to the other side. In a rhythm section, jumps are spaced so riders can **manoeuvre** through it smoothly. Sharp **banks** let racers take corners without slowing down.

FREESTYLE

BMX racing quickly led to BMX freestyle riding. In BMX freestyle, riders soar off large jumps. They perform stunts in the air.

manoeuvre move in a planned and controlled way

bank angle of the track; if a track has a high bank, the top of the track is much higher than the bottom of the track

FACT
BMX bikes do not have kickstands.
Racers do not need them and they
only add extra weight to the bike.

17

CHAPTER 3
Basic rules

It is against the rules to bump other riders on purpose to make them crash or slow down. But BMX riders often bump into one another by accident.

Rules guide other parts of a race too. On the final stretch, a racer cannot block another racer who may have more speed built up. If a racer accidentally leaves the track, that racer must re-enter the track as soon as it is safely possible.

"You can reach your goal if you believe in your dreams."

– *BMX Olympic gold medalist Mariana Pajón*

FACT

Mariana Pajón began racing BMX bikes when she was 4 years old. She competed for Colombia in the 2012 and 2016 Olympics and won the gold medal both times.

CHAPTER 4

Riding tips

Now that you're ready to ride, you can give it a try. These riding tips can help you race for first place.

STARTING GATE

Being fast out of the starting gate can give you a great advantage. Try starting with both feet on the pedals while balancing, so when the gate drops you'll be ready to go.

JUMPS

It may be tempting to try to jump as high as you can, but low jumps keep up your speed.

LANDING

When tracks have a series of jumps, try to land on the downward slope of a jump. You'll keep up your speed.

WARM UP

Make sure you're warmed up and stretched before a race so you are ready to give it your all.

FACT

Rear brakes are best for BMX races. Front brakes could cause the bike to flip.

21

Glossary

bank   angle of the track; if a track has a high bank, the top of the track is much higher than the bottom of the track

frame   main part of the bicycle to which other parts are attached

gear   toothed wheel that is connected to another toothed wheel; gears can be changed to control the amount of roll out or force applied by pedalling

manoeuvre   move in a planned and controlled way

obstacle   something a BMX rider jumps or rides over

qualification heat   one of several early races that determine which riders advance to future qualifying rounds or the main event

starting gate   place where a race starts; the gate accommodates eight riders and ensures that all riders get a fair start

wipeout   fall or crash

Read more

Cycling (Usborne Spectator Guides), Katie Daynes (Usborne Publishing Ltd, 2016)

Extreme Sports, Emily Bone (Usborne Publishing Ltd, 2014)

Wheel Sports (Extreme Sports) Michael Hurley (Raintree, 2011)

Websites

www.bbc.co.uk/sport
Read about the latest news in sport!

www.britishcycling.org.uk/bmx
Visit the official website for the British Cycling Federation.

www.dkfindout.com/uk/sports/cycling
Learn important facts about cycling.

Index